The California Gold Rush

R. Conrad Stein

CHILDRENS PRESS®
CHICAGO

Library of Congress Cataloging-in-Publication Data

Stein, R. Conrad.
    The California gold rush / by R. Conrad Stein.
        p. cm. — (Cornerstones of freedom)
    ISBN 0-516-06691-9
    1. California—Gold discoveries—Juvenile literature.
I. Title. II. Series.
F865.S8192 1995
979.4'01—dc20   94-38651
                                                      CIP
                                                       AC

John Augustus Sutter was a failure as a businessman in Switzerland and fled to the United States in 1834 to escape his many debts. He drifted from state to state and wound up in California in 1839. With these meager beginnings, John Sutter appeared an unlikely figure to be remembered in history books. But eventually he played a key role in launching the great California Gold Rush of 1849.

John Sutter

When Sutter arrived in the West, the huge territory of California belonged to Mexico. The Mexican settlements there amounted to a handful of missions near the village of Los Angeles and the shores of San Francisco Bay. After Sutter arrived, he talked the Mexican governor into giving him 50,000 acres of land in the Sacramento Valley. Sutter now believed that with so much land under his control, he could become wealthy and powerful.

Sutter's mill on the American River

The Mexican-American War soon broke out as the United States battled Mexico for the rights to territory in the West. Mexico lost the war in 1848 and surrendered a vast region of land to the United States, including California.

John Sutter, meanwhile, paid little attention to the war. A dream churned in his mind. He hoped to acquire still more land and establish his own empire in California. He had built a fort near the American River and now called himself "Captain Sutter." Several hundred people lived and worked within the walls of his fort, where Sutter raised livestock and grew crops.

James Marshall (right) and his cabin (left). Marshall's discovery of gold nuggets touched off the California Gold Rush.

James Marshall was a foreman overseeing the construction of Sutter's sawmill on the American River. On January 24, 1848, Marshall saw a glint of yellow in the river where the ground had been dug up. He bent over and picked up several tiny nuggets. They were no bigger than kernels of corn. He suddenly realized that he might have found gold. A few days later, after finding more yellow nuggets, an excited Marshall appeared in John Sutter's office.

Marshall showed the tiny gold pieces to Sutter. They tested the metal to make sure it was gold. After boiling a nugget in a kettle of lye, the gold rock emerged intact. Now the two men were sure they had discovered gold. Sutter grinned. Gold on his property could make him even richer and more powerful than he had dared to dream.

Sutter and Marshall attempt to contain their excitement as they survey the land that they know contains valuable gold.

Sutter tried to keep the discovery a secret, but the news soon leaked out. Through gossip and rumor, Sutter's secret spread throughout the entire Sacramento Valley. A month later, news of gold at Sutter's mill "in considerable quantities" appeared in a small newspaper called the *Californian*. Almost immediately, gold fever swept through California like an epidemic. Men dropped what they were doing and rushed to Sutter's mill. Farmers left plows in the fields. Store owners bolted their doors shut. Even the newspaper that had broken the story shut down. The reporters and pressmen of the *Californian* ran off to dig for gold.

These people were overcome with the powerful lure of gold. They fantasized that becoming a miner was a simple way to get extremely rich. They thought that any able-bodied person with a shovel and a pan could strike a "motherlode"—a huge deposit of gold. Indeed, those who arrived first did strike it rich. A man named Joe Dye collected $40,000 of gold in just seven weeks. Two partners, William Daylor and Perry McCoon, made $17,000 in one week. A twelve-year-old boy found $2,700 worth of gold in just two days.

A CALIFORNIA MINER.

A typical miner did not need much more than a shovel, a pan, and a pickax in the California Gold Rush.

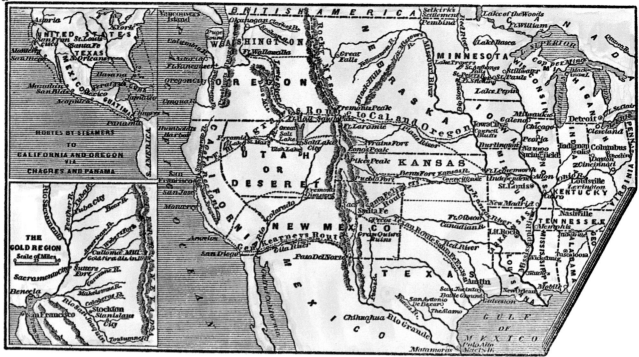

In the mid-1800s, people from the eastern states headed west of the Mississippi River and swarmed over the western frontier.

News of the California gold strike spread east. Hunters and traders heading eastward across the Great Plains talked to settlers on the Mississippi River. Sailors who had shipped out of San Francisco brought stories to cities on the Atlantic coast. They told wild tales of the ground in California littered with huge chunks of gold, and of men who had become millionaires overnight. The stories were exaggerated, but they were based on truth. There *were* fortunes to be made in California.

The gold found at Sutter's mill caused one of the wildest mass movements of people the world had ever seen. In 1849, thousands of people from farms, small towns, and cities of the eastern United States headed to California.

The 85,000 gold seekers who reached California in 1849 were nicknamed "forty-niners." These included young men looking for adventure, as well as older men who had deserted their families in search of an instant fortune.

And the forty-niners were virtually all men. Women were so rare in California that men were known to travel miles just to gaze at one. Few women actually mined for gold. Most of the women in California were wives of miners, keepers of boardinghouses, entertainers, cooks, or prostitutes. Even by 1850, women made up only eight percent of the California population.

A rare sight in the goldfields: a woman (second from left) brings lunch to miners.

The first decision a forty-niner faced was how to get to California. He could choose from several routes. One choice was to take a ship out of an Atlantic port, sail around Cape Horn at the tip of South America, and then go up the Pacific coast to San Francisco. The journey took at least six months, and it was far from a pleasant cruise. Greedy ship captains signed up as many passengers as they could cram into their vessels, and the men often slept three to a bed. At Cape Horn, violent storms tossed ships like toy boats in a bathtub. Many forty-niners became so seasick they cursed the day they decided to seek gold.

FOR
CALIFORNIA!
Mutual Protection
Trading & Mining Co.

Having purchased the splendid, Coppered and very fast Sailing
Barque EMMA ISIDORA,
Will leave about the 15th of February. This vessel will be fitted in the very best manner and is one of the fastest sailing vessels that goes from this port.

Each member pays 300 dollars and is entitled to an equal proportion of all profits made by the company either at mining or trading, and holds an equal share of all the property belonging to the company. Experienced men well acquainted with the coast and climate are already engaged as officers of the Company. A rare chance is offered to any wishing a safe investment, good home and Large profits.

This Company is limited to 60 and any wishing to improve this opportunity must make immediate application.

An Experienced Physician will go with the company.

For Freight or Passage apply to 23 State Street, corner of Devonshire, where the list of Passengers may be seen.

JAMES H. PRINCE, Agent,
23 State Street, corner of Devonshire St., Boston.
For further Particulars, see the Constitution.   Propeller Power Press, 142 Washington St., Boston.

Profit-hungry ship companies printed advertisements (above) that lured easterners to the goldfields of California. So many people responded to the lure of gold that ships were terribly overcrowded (right).

Another route west was to take a ship to Mexico or Panama, cross overland, and then take another ship north to California. Crossing Panama meant a long trip through mosquito-infested swamps. Dozens of miners caught malaria there and died.

Some miners hired native boatmen in Panama to paddle them through the maze of rivers that cut from one side of the country to the other. These boatmen were in such great demand that their fees rose from ten to fifty dollars in just a few months.

Hopeful miners land at Panama, which was only halfway through their journey west.

The most popular route west ran overland. Forty-niners gathered at frontier settlements such as St. Joseph on the Missouri River. From there, they headed west by horse, wagon, mule, or even on foot. They followed almost the same route taken by explorers Lewis and Clark a half-century earlier. But these ill-equipped travelers encountered a perilous journey. After passing

through the Great Plains, the forty-niners had trouble finding water and grass for their animals. Near the Sierra Nevada mountains, they faced a hellish stretch of land called the Forty-Mile Desert. One forty-niner wrote to a friend who was preparing for the trip, "Expect to find the worst desert you ever saw, and then find it worse than you expected."

The California Gold Rush of 1849 was just part of a massive movement to the West by millions of people in the East. Families of homesteaders were also racing to the plains to establish farms. Ranchers staked out acres of land on which they raised cattle. Thousands of people went west to build a transcontinental railroad to connect the eastern cities with the western frontier. When this railroad was completed in 1869, the door opened for millions more newcomers.

Thousands of easterners journeyed west in the 1800s. The trip proved perilous and even deadly to many of the travelers, who were unprepared for the rough journey and the awful weather.

CAMPERS NEAR BOULDER

A tragic part of the United States' western expansion was its devastating effect on Native Americans. The arriving easterners disrupted almost every aspect of life for these people, who had lived in these regions for centuries. Cowboys hunted buffalo nearly to the point of extinction, robbing the Indians of a primary food source. The miners in California and other territories forced Indians (as well as Hispanics) off land

Many gold seekers were unwelcome intruders on the land of American Indians.

The invasion by whites from the East permanently destroyed the lifestyles that native Indian communities had established centuries before.

they had lived on for generations. These new-comers also brought diseases, such as measles, to which the Indians had never been exposed. Some tribes were destroyed by epidemics that swept through their communities. Many Indian tribes stood up and fought the whites, continuing years of vicious, bloody conflict.

If a forty-niner survived the perilous journey west, he arrived in California to find a bizarre society based on one thing only—the greedy,

A pan was a miner's most valuable possession.

frenzied pursuit of gold. A new arrival was probably first struck by the incredible prices he would have to pay for most goods. Merchants quickly discovered they could charge miners outrageous prices and get away with it. A store owner named Sam Brannan learned that miners used iron pans to take gold from streambeds. Brannan bought practically every iron pan in California at 20¢ apiece. He then resold the pans to forty-niners for $8 or more, making himself a millionaire. Before 1849, a horse might have sold for $6 in California; now it cost a whopping $300. And the price of food was enough to make a miner cry. A loaf of bread cost $2. A pound of butter—$6. One egg—$3. A tin of sardines—$16.

The forty-niners learned another quick lesson: gold mining was extremely hard work. The simplest way a person could mine was to "pan" for gold by scooping dirt from a riverbed into a round pan with a flat bottom. By gently swirling water in the pan, he washed the dirt over the edge, leaving gold dust and flakes behind. Gold is a heavy metal, so it settled at the bottom of the pan. Panning was an effective technique, but it was slow, backbreaking work. A miner spent hours squatting in an ice-cold stream with his hands underwater. At the end of a long day, his arms might be numb up to the elbows.

Most miners panned for gold dust or gold flakes, but they all dreamed of striking it rich by finding large nuggets. Nuggets were usually very small lumps of gold weighing only a few, precious ounces. On rare occasions, huge nuggets were found that weighed several pounds. The largest single nugget ever found in the United States was dug out of the California goldfields in the mid-1850s. This monster weighed an incredible 159 pounds.

Miners hunt for gold in a deep riverbed (above). Most miners collected tiny amounts of gold dust, but others were lucky enough to find nuggets (below).

A miner rocks the cradle while his partner brings more water and dirt.

The methods used by miners were constantly being revised and improved. By 1850, many miners were using a cradle, or rocker, which was a simple machine that operated on the same principle as panning. The cradle consisted of a wooden box with an open bottom. The bottom was covered by a perforated metal screen. One man would shovel dirt into the box, another added water, and a third rocked it. The rocking motion sifted the gold to the bottom, where it fell through the screen and was collected in a tarp or box below.

The next development was the long tom, a wooden trough several feet long. Miners shoveled dirt into the trough, and water washed it down to a perforated screen. The smallest pieces of dirt and gold were sifted into a box with indentations carved into its base. The gold would collect in the indentations, or cleats. The long tom was eventually expanded upon, becoming the sluice. The sluice was a series of connected long boxes. Water from a stream was directed into the top of the sluice, which ran downhill. Several men stood along the sluice

Miners working a long tom

Miners searched for gold in fields and mountainsides (bottom), as well as riverbeds (right). Below, two miners "winnow" for gold by scooping dirt into a blanket and tossing it into the air; the dirt would blow away, and the gold would drop into the blanket.

and shoveled dirt into it. Water washed the dirt away and gold collected in cleats cut in the base of the sluice boxes.

Each of these improvements on mining methods allowed the miners to collect more gold in less time. But as their machines grew larger and more complex, the miners needed to work together with more men. Many formed partnerships or hired workers, but these relationships often went sour. Vicious arguments erupted over how to divide the gold into fair shares. Disputes often ended in brutal fights, and even in murder. At the height of the gold rush, about two murders a day took place in San Francisco. Vigilante groups sometimes hunted and punished suspected criminals. Since there was no established system of justice, the criminals were often hung without a trial.

Mining with a sluice; the water is supplied by a "flutter-wheel," which is turned by the river's current.

San Francisco grew rapidly in its days as a gold-rush boomtown.

Whenever a new gold strike was found, it was impossible to keep the news a secret. The telephone had not been invented, but rumors somehow spread like lightning. When miners found gold, they marked off their "claim" to that plot of land. The understood law was that nobody could mine on another man's claim. But that did not stop miners from swarming to the area and staking nearby claims.

Wherever a large quantity of gold was found, instant communities appeared consisting of tents and rickety shacks, called shanties. If it turned out there wasn't much gold to be had at that location, the "shantytown" quickly disappeared.

But if the strike was big, a "boomtown" was born. The town was given a name, and buildings were constructed quickly to house a blacksmith, a bank, a church, and a general store.

The biggest, busiest, and wildest boomtown in California was San Francisco. Before the gold rush, San Francisco was a tiny fort of 400 settlers. In two years, the population soared to 25,000. Streets were built over fields where cows had grazed peacefully only a few weeks earlier. Thirty new houses were constructed each day. And to satisfy the entertainment needs of the men who swarmed to the city, there were hundreds of saloons and gambling houses.

Philip Armour

In boomtowns, many people became rich even without digging for gold. Businessmen who came west to trade with miners were sometimes more successful than the miners, themselves. Twenty-year-old Philip Armour came to California believing that beef was more important than gold. Armour opened a butcher shop and sold meat to miners. Armour's business grew rapidly, and he eventually became the largest supplier of beef in the United States. Another businessman who got his start in California was Levi Strauss. He was successful selling denim pants that were strong enough to withstand the miners' rough work. These pants became known as jeans and eventually became a staple of American clothing. "Levi's" are still popular today.

Levi Strauss

And what of John Augustus Sutter, the man who was there when the gold rush began? By the time the gold rush was in full swing, Sutter's 50,000 acres of land were overrun with miners. They trampled his crops and orchards, muddied his streams, and slaughtered his cattle for food. "The country swarmed with lawless men," Sutter later wrote. "Talking with them did no good. I was alone and there was no law." Since he could not fight the waves of miners, Sutter decided to join them. Discarding his dreams of an empire, he bought mining gear and set out for the hills. He was unlucky, however, and never struck it rich. Years later, Sutter went to Washington, D.C., to reclaim his land in California. He appealed to Congress to recognize his claim to the land that Mexico had given him. On June 18, 1880, while

John Sutter lost control of his land when it was taken over by countless miners.

Congress was considering his request, John Sutter
died in a Washington hotel room.

The California Gold Rush was brief and
furious. It began in 1848 and swept the nation
in 1849. In 1850, California was admitted to
the Union because of its huge population, and
because it was so rich in gold profits. But the
influx of gold seekers was already beginning to
decline by 1851. Individual miners with pans
and pickaxes could only get at the gold that was
near the earth's surface and in riverbeds. By
1855, almost all the miners had vacated
California and were hunting for gold and silver
in other territories. Major gold rushes brought
swarms of miners to such places as Tombstone,
Arizona; Pikes Peak, Colorado; and Deadwood,
South Dakota. Everywhere a gold rush hit, the

*Denver, Colorado
(left), was founded
when gold was
discovered there
in 1858. It grew
rapidly during the
nearby Pikes Peak
gold rush of 1859.*

Some ghost towns still stand on the sites of boom-towns from more than a century ago.

same pattern was repeated. Boomtowns suddenly appeared, but they often turned into ghost towns when the miners disappeared. They left behind eerie, empty buildings. Remnants of some of these towns still stand in western states. Today, they are popular tourist attractions.

Individual miners abandoned California in the early 1850s, but there was still gold to be had. It was buried deep in the ground. Almost as quickly as the forty-niners had arrived, large mining companies moved in and began using large machinery to get at more gold. One new technique they developed was hydraulic mining,

Hydraulic mining proved too damaging to the environment, so it was eventually banned.

in which powerful jets of water were sprayed against mountainsides to wash out the gold. This left the landscape pocked and rutted, and nearby rivers became clogged with the runoff silt. The environmental damage caused by hydraulic mining was so severe that the practice was banned in 1884. But the mining industry continued to flourish, and gold and silver are still mined successfully in the West.

The California Gold Rush played a key role in launching the American mining industry. At the time miners flocked to the West with gold fever, huge coal deposits were starting to be mined in Pennsylvania. Today, mining for such resources as gold, silver, coal, lead, tin, copper, salt, and petroleum are important industries in the United States.

Among the forty-niners who rushed to California in search of fortunes, only a few became instant millionaires. And for every one millionaire, there were a thousand failures whose lives were crushed by the disappointment. So many gambled on making a fortune and lost.

But many of these losers did not give up their dreams of a fortune in gold. Throughout the 1850s, many raced across the American frontier searching for another big strike. As those incurable miners left California they sang a hopeful song to the tune of "Oh Susanna!":

Farewell, Old California,
I'm going far away.
Where gold is found more plenty,
In larger lumps they say.

A gold-rush miner alone in his cabin

GLOSSARY

Cradle

Panning

boomtown – a town that grew suddenly near a gold strike

claim – a piece of land that a miner said he owned

cradle – a wooden box that was rocked to separate gold from dirt and rocks

denim – a strong, cotton cloth used to make jeans

epidemic – a fast-spreading disease

foreman – the supervisor of a crew of workers

forty-niner – a person who went to California in 1849 looking for gold

frontier – the unexplored edge of a settled region; in the early and mid-1800s, the western frontier of the United States included most of the land west of the Mississippi River

homesteader – a person who moved west to establish a farm

hydraulic mining – a mining technique in which powerful jets of water were blasted against mountains to loosen gold from the rocks

long tom – a long box used to separate gold from dirt and rocks

lye – an abrasive liquid used in making soap

mission – a local church established to promote a religion or faith in a specific region; Catholic missions in California attempted to convert American Indians to Christianity

panning – a mining technique in which dirt and water were combined in a flat, round pan; the dirt washed over the edges, and gold settled in the bottom of the pan

perforated – when holes are punched in a flat surface

shanty – a shack

sluice – a series of connected narrow boxes; miners directed water into the sluice to separate gold from rocks and dirt

transcontinental railroad – a railroad system that reaches across a continent; the first transcontinental railroad in North America was completed in 1869

TIMELINE

The Louisiana Purchase **1803**

Lewis and Clark reach the Pacific Ocean **1805**

1834

John Sutter emigrates
to the United States

Sutter settles in California **1839**

1845 Texas becomes an American state

1846
} The Mexican-American War
1848

1849

1850 California becomes a state

Gold discovered
at Sutter's mill

1859 Gold rush at Pikes Peak, Colorado

1861
U.S. Homestead Act **1862** } U.S. Civil War
1865

1869 Transcontinental railroad completed

1876 Gold rush at Deadwood, South Dakota

1880 John Sutter dies in Washington, D.C.

Forty-niners rush
to California

INDEX (*Boldface* page numbers indicate illustrations.)

PHOTO CREDITS

ADDITIONAL PICTURE IDENTIFICATION
Page 2: *Sutter's mill under construction — where James Marshall first found gold*

STAFF

Project Editor: Mark Friedman
Design & Electronic Composition: TJS Design
Photo Editor: Jan Izzo
Cornerstones of Freedom Logo: David Cunningham

ABOUT THE AUTHOR
R. Conrad Stein was born and grew up in Chicago. After serving in the U.S. Marine Corps, he attended the University of Illlinois, where he earned a B.A. in history. He later studied in Mexico, where he received an advanced degree in fine arts.

Reading history is Mr. Stein's hobby. He tries to bring the excitement of history to his work. Mr. Stein has published many history books for young readers. He lives in Chicago with his wife and their daughter, Janna.